VISION AND THE VOICE

Watch the film at
TheSyncBook.com/VAV

SYNC BOOK RADIO MOVIE

Film Transcript

VISION AND THE VOICE

05.03.18

thesyncbook.com/VAV

That's what's happening to us;

It is the breakdown of reality.

And isn't that what we do? Isn't that what explorers of the so-called "Sync" phenomenon do?

We break things down.

I've been on this planet for 40 years
and I'm no closer to understanding a single thing.

When trying to appreciate a meaning, you need to go back to the beginning. It's just like reading a book, you know, you need to start a book at the beginning.

And this is one of the things about Sync that I feel has a slightly sinister twist to it, is that, you enter into it, it's like a gyroscope, you know? And you can't really know what the beginning is.

Why am I here, how did I get here?

Another great thinker who talks about this is Robert Anton Wilson. He talks about the concept of just sitting—and this is an exercise that everyone should do. You just start thinking about how you got where you are, and in a very specific sense, like, "How did I get into this chair?" basically, and you go backwards from there. And you keep going backwards, and you keep going backwards, and you don't stop until you can tell everything about how you got into this chair, and inevitably, you'll end up at the concept of the first cause.

Go back, to the beginning.

*WHAT'S TAKING
PLACE RIGHT NOW
IS IMPOSSIBLE.*

*IT CAN'T POSSIBLY BE
HAPPENING.*

*AND,
IF YOU THINK ABOUT
THE BEGINNING
OF THINGS,
YOU'LL SEE THIS.*

Isn't it a weird impulse, when you think about it, to take one kind of experience, and translate it into another kind of experience?

Indeed.

And why, in heavens name, would you want to take something that was made for the ear and translate it into a very abstract sense, the eye? Because with the ear you get vibrations, you get feelings, you get movement, you get touch, you get kinesis as well as hearing. But, when you write it down, there's only one sense responding, the eye.

Correct.

And you can close your eyes.

Right.

But it's the only sense with lids.
    You don't have earlids.

Right, it is the only sense with lids.

Yeah, the only one you can turn on and off.
    All the others are on 24/7

SEE ME

FEEL ME

TOUCH ME

HEAL ME

I think this has to do with the hierarchy of our senses. We are obsessed by the eyes. The Panopticon, the Spectacle—you know the political order on one side, where you see, and this is Foucault, and on the other side, the sort of oppression by spectacle—is both linked to the eye.

But if we attach importance to the other senses, touch, and ear and hearing. Then, you relate to the invisible. And I think this is where things are happening now, in the invisible.

As soon as, and this is why I love radio, it's immediately striking the way words sound differently, when they're shown, when they're put on stage.

There is the cinema, that is overwhelming; there is video gaming now—has to do with the Debord and the sort of fictional intoxication in which we are maintained. If you compare it to the other art form, which is books—in a way books are much more dangerous because they maintain this *invisibleness*. And they maintain this, you know relation, with what is not seen, with what can't be shown.

And the Western way doesn't bear this, they can't cope with it.

They have to see.

They have to see *everything*.

In essence, it's a hieroglyphic film. The film is poured into your brain, it's not . . . um, laser beamed into your brain. That it engages different parts of the brain. And unless you regularly utilize those, you're gonna reject it.

There's a whole limited view of films and books in the first place. The way that we receive something is always our own. We go through our lives judging everything as if our perception was the reality.

When you remove all the veils and get to just the literalest of literalisms, that's the secret of *2001*. The monolith is the screen, the theater is the cube. They have you inside of the place that they are showing you.

It's weird that we take on this role, that we're going to just watch something, and meanwhile we're creating it at the same time, with our relationship to the imagery, and lampoon characters, and everything.

You actually step into it, it's a place, it is your brain, it's like the two mirrors, if you get the angles just correct, then you see infinity. *Reflection upon reflection upon reflection.* It is a technology, it is not literature.

It's an interactive thing, we're not spectators here.

I hear nothing.

Okay so, in *2001*, the whole thing about the monolith is that when it's finally turned on its side, Bowman enters the Stargate, correct? And that's the whole, "oh the monolith was the film screen."

Right.

Okay well, as you build a tower from ground up, against gravity, due to the constraints of physics and the way the world is, at a certain point, that tower is just destined to fall. But if you conceive of the tower of language as being on its side, well then you have, basically, an encyclopedia.

So the tower, if you, if the fault of what the past was, the old consciousness was, the animal consciousness, the very phallic consciousness was that we're gonna fuck the sky. We're gonna build the biggest phallus that we can and we're gonna fuck the sky and we give birth to whatever it is.

But really a more intelligent person knows that no, that the tower is the story of history and that a new foundation needs to be built for even a horizontal story. So how do you create a foundation in that manner?

And that is, well that's the whole mystery to me is, how do you reset history?

I felt for many, many years that the world is made of language but that there's more to it than that. It's that everything is code. Everything is code in the sense that hackers mean when they say they write code.

That the universe is a puzzle. Life is a problem to be solved, it's a conundrum. It's not what it appears to be. There are doors, there are locks and keys. There are levels. And if you get it right, somehow it will give way to something extremely unexpected.

The ancient Jews used Hebrew as their numerical system. Each letter's a number. Like the Hebrew A, aleph, one. B, bet, it's two. Torah's just a long string of numbers. Some say that it's a code sent to us from God.

These letters are the building blocks of subsequent creation. Each letter is a channel to a particular energy. Binah combines these into words and phrases, spelling out new worlds and their inhabitants as we read in Genesis.

If you learn how to properly blow a smoke ring, the smoke ring deteriorates into the letters of the Hebrew alphabet.

Everything deteriorates into the letters of the Hebrew alph—

OK well.

When I was in India, I came across a scene where these groups of people were having this argument. I thought they were pissed at each other. And the Indian man who I was with basically expressed to me that those are Samkhyists and those are Vedantists and they've been having this debate forever. And they get excited, and their visualization skills get activated because they're so excited because they're having this communication. Basically they open themselves up to the realm of possibilities and they're not mad at each other, they're just considering it from every fucking possible angle. So it's a good debate.

I'm gonna say honestly, I don't feel like I know what the truth is. I feel like I have a concept of it but it's really hard to talk about things at all. In any voice either the written voice or the spoken voice without sounding like you think you are actually speaking some kind of truth. It's just kind of a never ending puzzle.

When I first discovered James Joyce I wanted to read Finnegan's Wake right away. By the time I was halfway, not even halfway, I won't even lie, by the time I was a quarter of the way through the first so-called sentence I thought what the fuck is this man? What the hell am I supposed to do with this? So I went to the library and I got out this book, it was five times longer than Finnegan's Wake. And in it I read, I just started flipping through the pages and I went oh my God, there's no way I'm ever gonna understand this. There's no way.

> Isn't that the way we really should appreciate reality? That when we have our first taste of reality it should just be so monumentally dense, bizarre and confusing that we should just run to anybody in proximity and say what the fuck is going on?

Absolutely yes I agree.

> Right and the problem is is that when you do that they say "I don't know! I was hoping you knew what the fuck was going on."

>> Or the other problem is that someone says "oh I know, let me tell you. Here's a bible or here's a textbook or here's whatever, we've got the answers, just trust me."

You think that there's actually something to find that's gonna stand out at the end of your fucking search to find yourself. You can't find yourself, you never lost yourself. It's insane.

I will always be here

Time is an ocean

I will always look out from behind these eyes

Space is a puff of smoke, a wisp of cloud

It's only a lifetime

Your mind . . .

It's only a lifetime

. . . hovering through all the possibilities

It's only a lifetime

It's about agency in a space where there's no agency at all. Like if you're a character in a story what do you do with that?

So what do you do with that?

You go off the page.

We teach them through something called contrastive stress drills. And so what you do is you take a single sentence like I have a car and each word gets emphasis and it changes the meaning of the sentence. *I* have a car, not you. I *have* a car, I don't want one. Or you know I have a *car*. And so each time you emphasize those there's subtext as a result of the tonal change, the prosody underneath.

It's all in the mind.

We can talk about musical form. You know you can take pretty much any sort of content, I mean like classical like sonata form is about taking whatever melodic fragments you have and put 'em into this machine that turns it into five minutes of music. You're gonna take this little thing and then you're gonna go through this musical process and arrive at this secondary little thing.

Funny you're using navigational language to describe it.

Right yeah.   Of motion.

Right and then you're gonna come back at the end and you're going to put it through this other musical process, it's gonna end up in a different place and you have these milestones around the way that tell you that you've done it right or wrong and it's kind of content blind. You can do this with any input.

So it's great that you kept relying really while you were speaking really rapidly to talk about sonata form, you were relying on words that we also rely on to talk about moving through physical space right? And as if you're navigating. Every time you are forced to make choice about the way you interpret something that you store up here, with what it's gonna lead you to out here, you're making a choice physically which direction to navigate to, which is the language that you just described to navigate inside your own head through the form of a piece of music. And that's a series of negotiations that's building this scaffolding that you described earlier for each person. And at any moment two people might land on the same nodes and maybe they think that they're standing on the internal version, and the other one thinks they're standing on the external version, and something happens, and then Siri starts talking to you.

Yeah, a lot of that going on these days.

And I'm not necessarily asserting that this is what's happening, but what better way do I have to work it out than talk through it with language?

You're so brainwashed.

I'm a victim brother.

A victim.

Yeah, I'm a victim of 400 years of conditioning.

Shut up.

The man has programmed my condition.

Mm hmm.

Even my conditioning has been conditioned.

He was a radio guy in New York back in the '30s and '40s and '50s. One night he was lying there in bed and all of a sudden he found himself bumping up against something. And he thought 'this is strange I didn't know I'd fallen out of bed.' And he realized what he was bumping up against was the ceiling. And so as that realization turned around, looked down, and there in bed next to his wife was a gentleman and all of a sudden he realized that the man was himself. So he thought he had died. 'Oh I've got to get back in my body.' And at the thought of getting back in his body, bam, there he was.

And that was the first experience. And of course it scared him to death. He thought he was either going crazy or he was about ready to die and so forth. Meanwhile as he was looking into the effects of sound on consciousness and sleep and he went well, 'I wonder if I can recreate this out of body state.' The sound became later known as hemi-sync. Short for hemispheric synchronization.

What he found was he was able to cause a frequency following response in the brain. He was using sound, one sound in one ear, let's say 100 hertz and 103 hertz in the other ear and then the brain acts like a mixer and it produces this third tone, the three hertz differential. And so it's kind of an entrainment effect. You start learning how to get into these different effects with the use of sound.

They work with silhouettes. You see an airplane in the sky far off and you can't make out details, just silhouette immediately you'll ask is it *Tommy can you hear me* coming towards me or going away *Can you feel me near you* And it could be either. *Tommy can you see me* You may have to watch it for a while. *Can I help to cheer you*

If this is a dream, which all the wisdom traditions teachings are saying, yeah this isn't metaphorically *like* a dream, this *is* a dream. If I'm split off from my own darkness, I'm gonna project it outside of myself in the dream. And then what is the dream gonna do but just to reflect back that very state. So then into the dream is gonna walk somebody who's embodying the shadow that I've split off from myself and projected outside of myself. And they're gonna be playing out the shadow.

And if I'm not aware that that's just a reflection of my own split off darkness, now I have evidence that the shadow really is outside of myself. So then I become even more entrenched in my point of view that the evil is outside of myself so then I even more project it, project the shadow outside of myself. Of course the more I do that the more it gets incarnate and embodied seemingly outside of myself in a self perpetuating feedback loop.

Will I dream?

And so then what do I do? I then try to destroy the very evil I see out there which is a reflection of the original inner process of trying to get rid of my own shadow. So I'm actually playing out in the outside world my inner process, and by doing that, by trying to destroy the evil out there, I'm actually becoming possessed by the evil I'm trying to destroy. And of course they're probably doing the same thing to me, it's a co-dreaming process.

The Shadow knows

We live inside a dream

Marine, what is that button on your body armor? A peace symbol sir! What is that you've got written on your helmet? Born to kill, sir! You write born to kill on your helmet and you wear a peace button. What's that supposed to be, some kind of sick joke? No sir! What is it supposed to mean? I think I was trying to suggest something about the duality of man, sir! What? The duality of man, the Jungian thing, sir!

I remember everything! I remember every little thing as if it happened only yesterday. I was barely 17, and I once killed a boy with a Fender guitar. I don't remember if it was a Telecaster or a Stratocaster but I do remember that it had a heart of chrome and a voice like a horny angel! I don't remember if it was a Telecaster or a Stratocaster but I do remember that it wasn't at all easy. It required the perfect combination of the right power chords and the precise angles from which to strike. The guitar bled for about a week afterward and the blood was sooth dark and rich like wild berries. The blood of the guitar was Chuck Berry red! The guitar bled for about a week afterward but it rung out beautifully. And I was able to play notes that I had never even heard before.

It's a land that God, if he exists, has created in anger, taking a close look at what's around us. There is some sort of a harmony. It's the harmony of overwhelming and collective murder. And we in comparison to the articulate vileness and baseness and obscenity of all this jungle, we in comparison to that enormous articulation, we only sound and look like badly pronounced and half finished sentences out of a stupid suburban novel, a cheap novel.

Atoms are just vibrations, extensions of the BIG NOTE

I think it was Pythagoras that said all is number but I also think that there was something to the effect that all is vibration, and so, instead of a big bang there was a big clang?

> Clang? Yeah at the beginning there was the word, and the word is sound.

The word is sound.

> Yeah.

Oh. Ahem. Well all right, this is a very very old idea. And it actually comes out of the book of Genesis in the bible. Starting with the opening words, "and God said, let there be light," he didn't actually say 'suppose we have some light here guys?' What apparently went on was God *spoke light*, and the word "light" and the actual event are one and the same. Ok. So the entire creation was regarded as speech. Right. A spoken text. And from that comes the idea of the two books, the book of Revelation that has been written down and the book of nature, which was spoken directly. And has manifested as actual nature. Yeah. Ok. This was the creation. So the creation was a speech. But the speech didn't—it wasn't a syntactical thing, subject, verb, predicate, object, direct and indirect and so on. The speeches in this case were the words, were huge amounts of things all at once. And I guess if you listened to it, the sound would be very much like the big bang.

I'm gonna make like this five hour movie where like I flash lights at people and they like wake up.

Some years ago I was waiting for a bus here in London and I was reading, Colin Wilson did a little book about Jung. The section I was reading was about synchronicity and it was about this one case that Jung had where one of his clients was about to get married. And he wasn't exactly sure about it. And he asked Jung, and Jung said, "Well let's consult the I-Ching, and see what it has to say."

And so they, threw their I-Ching. I forget the number of the hexogram, but I think it was called "The Marrying Maiden" or something like that, but basically the reading was one should not marry this maiden. So I don't know if the guy wound up marrying the woman or not but this was the message. So as I read that, I thought to myself... And I had... Long story short, I wound up coming to London after a marriage fell apart and I was leaving Los Angeles. And I was divorced and everything. I was blown across the Atlantic by my midlife crisis.

And so I'm here in London reading this book and I say to myself, "gee I wish Jung was around when I was wondering whether to get married or not." And as I said that I looked, let me just tell you, as I said that, the bus came to the bus stop, I looked up from the book, and who do I see getting off the bus? My ex wife.

Around that time I had a whole series of precognitive dreams, synchronicities around her, it was very strange.

Oh, Ok, Ok, as if that was Jeremy's answer? Yeah. Well it was a lot of things. It's Ok. I missed it, I guess you had to be there. Yeah. *I've been out walking I don't do too much talking these days These Days These days I seem to think a lot About the things that I forgot to do* Alan? Yeah baby? Where are we? Oh don't try that shit right now. Come on, really?

It it I—

It destroyed my life.

I'm laughing about something that destroyed your life. I agree with you, I think that our, our similarities begin with an experience of that magnitude.

Where I lose it and it comes back, and I lose it and it comes back and it's just like, you know if I want it I can get it, but if I don't want it and I ignore it then it doesn't overwhelm my life like it did.

There's definitely waves where it's like Jesus I can't deal with this. It tapers, you know what I mean? To where it's kinda leaving you alone a second. But it's always there like if you wanna acknowledge it you can. So it is, I mean it is a form of insanity to a certain extent, always seeing connections, like uncontrollably, do you know what I mean?

Yeah well that's where it was at for me for a while to a point where I was ignoring my family and my kids and it got that bad. Well once you see it you don't ever unsee it but you get immune to its grasp in certain ways. Whereas it kinda can consume you when the fire starts and you start writing and you start looking into things you just get so blown away by the beauty of it you can get lost staring at it.

You mean there are other sections?
Hmm? Oh yes of course.

Two for Evil Dead please.
That'll be two dollars.

What's wrong with you? What's wrong with everybody in this crazy place? Answer me, can't you talk? Can't you move? Answer me!

Vibration thread. You are light. You are sound.
Drift within. This is your body.

Why are you wearing that stupid bunny suit?
Why are you wearing that stupid man suit?

My job is to plumb the depths dredge up something from inside, something honest.

Take it off.
You will kindly remove your mask.

I gotta tell you, the life of the mind, there's no road map for that territory and exploring it can be painful. The sort of pain most people don't know anything about.

I want you to watch the movie screen.

I think I'm getting 'the fear'

Well I suppose it could be some sort of illusion.
Yes, maybe we're being made to see and hear what we hope to find.
No. No it's all wrong. This is more than 200 years ahead of our time.
Or it could be that time itself is suspended here.

Look upon me! I'll show you the life of the mind! Look upon me! I'll show you the life of the mind! I'll show you the life of the mind! I'll show you the life of the mind! I will show you the life of the mind!

Ok Ok I'm gonna just, there's my paranoia calling.

Did you get lost on the trip? Did you get trapped in memory? Did you forget? You brought your old mind games with you. Dreary old paranoias. You had to make it a bad trip.

Philip K Dick describes in The Divine Invasion Emmanuel's ability to enact the Pythagorean transformation, which is the ability to be everywhere at all times at once, but when you go into that state you cannot move because to move would be to destroy the state that you're in. So this is where fooling around with psychedelics without enough information can really do a lot of damage because on high high doses in favorable conditions, and I'll vouch for my own experience, I have attained that sort of state of mind. But it is so radically alien to the Western being that the minute that you approach that everywhere at all times at once and you gaze upon everything, it's just too god damn much. So the minute that you extricate yourself from that state, you just are every single movement, every single breath, every single thing you experience becomes the grinding reality that is our physical plane. And that is where the bad trip experience, in my estimation, manifests itself. Is that something that you would agree with?

> Dead on the money, absolutely. You've totally gotten it right. But what I would add to that is that the bad trip experience is the purpose of the drug itself.

I almost would agree with that.

> They want to put you, well not *they* I mean cause now that gets too weird, but the whole—it's a feedback experience.

Right. Infinite recursion is the bad trip. But that's also—

> Exactly. You got it.

That is a realization in itself of what consciousness is in the first place.

> There's the idea that no matter what it is, whether it's an obstacle or a reward—so sort of may I receive both the good things and the bad things as a challenge. You have to experience both the bad trip and the high.

Right. They ultimately cancel each other out, there's an equanimity that's necessary in order for realization.

WELL OK YOU SEE NOW TO ME . . .
RIGHT THERE, THINGS GOT A LITTLE
BIT IN THE REALM OF WHAT I WOULD
CALL "SOPHISTICATED."

And, go ahead, you have something on your mind here.

Um, No not really, I'm just over here trying to create my world and I hope everyone does pay attention to being very detailed in their creation. And my favorite line from the movie Inception, "Dream bigger darling."

You get to a point where you can process reality consciously, continuously and you can do it for a certain amount of time before you kind of crash and then you have to log off and give yourself some space and then you log on again.

Thought about the way he took on the sea
Thought about the way it all fell apart
Thought about the way he took on the sea
Thought about the way it all fell apart

What is the goal if we are a community or a movement or anything—

Oh but I don't know that we are, cause I think that we're just a group of interested researchers or—

I guess what I was gonna say is—

So it's funny cause this moment just clarified that for me.

Thought about the way he took on the sea
Thought about the way it all fell apart
Thought about the way he took on the ocean
Thought about the way
It all fell apart
It all fell apart
It all fell apart
It all fell apart

You go off the page.

Allowed me time to process and heal—

You built a community.

What's that?

You were at the, I mean you were kind of the figurehead of a real community that had organically grown. That's no easy task. That's something that's significant and that you should feel proud of. But yeah it's also healthy that you recognize the long term implications of that in terms of your larger relationship with the world at large, right?

Oh interesting, so what I was... Um, Huh. I was, I actually think of it in almost the opposite terms.

Oh really?

Is that I was in this position, I had this community, I had these friends, and I ultimately feel like I needed to, and I don't know how I could have gotten through the last year while still managing to do all this stuff. I honestly felt like it was necessary for me to take this time away. But I also do feel like I abandoned some people I left some people hanging. And it's just the nature of the beast, it's like, I had to step away.

Yep I did the same thing.

Yeah you know, so I hope people forgive me and it is what it is.

Yeah I walked away from miRthkon at the peak of its success and for multiple years before I'd moved, all of the people involved were basically still totally on call and willing at the drop of a hat to jump back on duty and do whatever I wanted them to do. But it's not appropriate for me to utilize those resources anymore Cause I don't even know what I want to do anymore and I feel like I'd be wasting their time.

Right.

And they were very understanding ultimately when it really came to the head that this is over.

You don't get to die on the cross and leave the heavy lifting

This is not the end.

You don't get to get on stage, yell "Wake up!"

This is not the beginning of the end.

but then just leave.

It is the breakdown of reality.

We've gotta think in four-dimensional rather than three-dimensional terms. But you know that's what underlies that quote from Bucky Fuller, I'm so fond of, "The Universe is non-simultaneously apprehended."

Meaning we can never see the whole universe at once?

Yeah the whole universe at once is a meaningless expression within special and general relativity. All we can say is this part of the universe, within the same inertial system we're in.

You mean there are other sections?
Hmm? Oh yes of course!

And this is a war, and this is a museum and this is a disease and this is an orgasm and this is a hamburger.

Everything is the same even if it's different.

Exactly. But our everyday mind forgets this. We think everything is separate, limited, I'm over here, you're over there, which is true. But it's not the whole truth because we're all connected. Because we are connected.

Sure sure sure sure sure sure sure, yeah.

Stream of
conscious
ness, baby
steps to
telepathy
with my
personal
narrative,
stuff
coming
from my
conscious
ness that's
just rapid
fire, you
know
rapid fire
for your
eyes.

And so do you see what's happening? The spiral is tightening as it goes faster and faster. The resonances are impinging. The thing is getting nuttier and nuttier and nuttier as computers link all cultures together, all informational barriers dissolve. Everything is becoming connected to everything else. Not only everything in the present moment, but all past moments as well are being drawn, compressed, squeezed towards the production of the transcendental object at the end of time which is nothing less than all time, all space shrunk down to an atomic dimension and handed back to us.

We look for all these reference points in order to identify ourselves and localize ourselves and it's completely compulsory and everything depends upon us building up this holographic model which is Babel, it's a mandala, it's not meant to be forever, it's just like Solomon's temple, it isn't meant to endure, that's why there's a warning to David for building it.

This isn't something to be built by human hands, there's another temple being built on another level that transcends anything that we could ever put our hands to, it doesn't mean we shouldn't necessarily ultimately do it because we're doing it. We just have to recognize that when we set out to do that that it is ultimately a futile mission. You're not gonna build the utopia with your hands cause it's something that is already ultimately beyond our perception.

Synchronicity is basically any event that resonates any other event. And basically everything resonates everything else. If I explain a synchronicity in a film, cause we're such a mediated society people relate to that, they understand that and we all share that so we can look at it, we can explain the movie or a scene from Star Wars or 2001 A Space Odyssey and people will generally know that because we're so aware of pop culture and then you can point out the synchronicity between that and another event, maybe a historical event or maybe a news piece, whatever it is and we can share that experience now.

Realizing oh yeah, this is just a different strain of Sync films, but really, I mean to me it speaks to me so much more than sort of—not that I don't love the other highly edited things, but this long-form dropping in a classic record that you're really familiar with, with an iconic film that you're really familiar with and seeing how they sync, is just it hits me on every level that I love.

> It seems like this was done in tandem. It seems like the architecture of these two works of art, it was designed, so you bring in that whole evolutionary debate, is there a creator or is it just flow? Is Dark Side of the Rainbow just the element of how our universe flows? Or is this a specific occasion where a band structured their album based on the architecture of a movie?

The dynamic you're describing, my experience from doing Radio8Ball, when I was doing the radio show and I would pick a CD at random, play it on shuffle function and that was how we got the answer. Random, like reach in to a box, my eyes closed, put it in, and it would all happen right there on the radio. And when someone got an answer that was so right, when we came back, invariably, they were sure that I had cheated. I learned very early on —cause there's an impulse when you're doing it to hope that a certain record gets picked as a certain answer. And you find out really quickly that if you do that you get bad syncs and The Pop Oracle fucks with you. But if you surrender to it and really do it the answers will come out so correct. So going to what you're talking about is the idea of authorship. I think the nature of sync, it makes us see authorship where like the only authorship is the Fibonacci sequence, are hardwired archetypal things in our consciousness that, you know it'll keep landing on the right spot as long as you are letting it.

Pushing what people could project was something I was interested in doing. Like in Room 237, I think some of the fun for me was seeing how far I can stretch the relationship between what was on screen and what people were talking about and what people saw. The way Jack Nicholson could represent Jack Nicholson, he could represent Jack Torrance. He could represent any of the interviewees who are speaking about him. Sometimes he even represented Stanley Kubrick just in a context that we put him in, in 237. And I was looking at that very much through the lens of the Kuleshov effect. But I was also genuinely amazed. Every connection I looked for, I was somehow able to find.

A lot of those I didn't want to give any explanation, I just wanted to see what you could see if you just traced down all those different parts. Broke the movie down into its atoms, as it were, or even within the screen. And I think that's a little different than say, the approach that Blakemore takes. Cause I think his approach is, I mean he's a broadcaster, you know a professional voice. I think words are a bit more important to him and I think like when all the press came out for Room 237, the documentary that we're both featured in, he and Weidner and and Cocks kinda grabbed the headlines because their points of view can be explained in one sentence. You can say well Blakemore says it's about the Indians. Cocks says it's about the Holocaust, Weidner says it's about the Moon landing ... so but it's text, text-based and therefore maybe a bit simpler. People can read that and understand it. But when you start talking about pure visuals you're gonna have to, it's gonna take a few essays to get your point across. Or just a picture which—

You can put a bunch of stuff on the air or in a record that are really not necessarily related to each other at all put them in connection with one another and if there's any way to do it, people will make a connection in their minds and they'll make it have a meaning. Often you'll just have little bits of content. And the meaning of the piece is built out of the juxtaposition of all these different little things.

Come and see   See into trees   Find the girl   While you can

Come closer and see   See into the dark

Just follow your eyes   Just follow your eyes

That's what's so endlessly interesting about appropriating all these bits of media and the sound bites and putting them back together, recontextualizing all that.

There's a self defense aspect to the whole thing. Here you are, you're this person, you're out in the world with your little psyche, and your little psyche all day long is combing all this advertising, and all this media stuff, you didn't really invite it, it's just coming in there all the time. These things are coming in on you and you turn back, you turn the barrage back on itself in some way.

You say that at some point, the real became an image and so social criticism became more like film criticism where we could speak about reality in the abstract and it was a way of participating, but not really having to be accountable to what was happening in the world.

Well yeah certainly. Which is only increasing, this sentiment of powerlessness. We don't have power when we're contained to just criticize images or the reality as image.

OK I can see that, I can sense that.

Was blind **It's funny how the colors of the real world only seem really real when you viddy them on the screen** *but now I see*

3:30 in the morning, with not a soul in sight. We sat four-deep at a traffic light, talking about how dumb and brainwashed some of our brothers and sisters are, while we waited for a green light to tell us when to go.

It will blur our perception of what's real and what's not real. And when that happens, it will be media that has been the tool that has basically told our subconscious that these things are possible and that's when in my opinion we'll experience this mass ascension of everyone believing in our own divinity, believing that we're Gods.

Ok Don't start with that magic blanket bullshit.

> It's not magic, it's just the way things are, Tommy. You and me and the air—are actually tiny particles that are swirling around together. Look right here you see?

Ok, but look at the cracks between these particles and the cracks we fall through, the holes of nothingness.

> *Exactly, because that's what I just experienced upstairs.*

> But look closer, there are tiny particles connecting the larger cubes.

Yeah and then tinier cracks between the connections.

> And even tinier connections.

And even tinier cracks.

> Yeah but if you look close enough you can't tell where my nose ends and space begins because they're unified.

The pines are the towers.

> See?

Pines, towers.

> *So what? You can't see any of this anyway.*
> *Do you see anything?*

No. But I want to debate this particle cube thing.

In Manhattan it looks like it's near the World Trade Center complex and I just kept looking and 'I dunno it's really near' and a little bit of research revealed that it was actually flush with the Twin Towers, this building. It's called The Millenium Hilton and it's actually intentionally designed to look like the *2001* Monolith, and this object, this black Monolith that, in the film, opens the Stargate, in 2001, is flush with the World Trade Center, the Twin Towers or the pyramids; and the synchronicity of a building representing the Stargate next to the twin pillars of Solomon's temple perhaps which you could see as the Holiest of Holies which has now come down and been destroyed and sort of think of it as a portal or a gateway. So it seemed to correlate with the idea of Kurt Russel landing on the pyramids, landing on the pillars, landing on the World Trade Center and him being the first person going through the Stargate. So we have a few pieces of media coming together and expressing this idea of 9/11 connected to the Stargate and this eventually evolved into what I called 'the 9/11 Mega Ritual' or 'the opening of the Stargate of cosmic consciousness.'

You never see anything anyway

Consciousness focusing on any particular event will by necessity be dramatic and our minds were sort of silenced on 9/11. Our usual pattern, our day to day lives were altered. The entire planet went out of their pattern, looked at one event, and what they were looking at was a symbolic pillar and a Pentagon and it seems like that was a ritual, a ritualistic event that has altered the flow of history.

'What is sync good for?'
And I didn't put anything there.

We are not saving lives.
We watch a lot of movies.

It's a tough one.
It's the question at the center of the movie.

Will I ever make art again?

In the music world today

The label booked the troubadour

For a stop on their campaign

And the resulting concert film

The featurette where the front man

Gets all nostalgic with his pain

And I hate that kind of star

The heroes aren't your heroes and the

Enemies remain

Today I authorized two operations in Iraq. I know that many of you are rightly concerned about any American military action in Iraq. Even limited strikes like these, I understand that. I ran for this office in part to end our war in Iraq and welcome our troops home. But when the lives of American citizens are at risk, we will take action. Earlier this week, one Iraqi in the area cried to the world, "there is no one coming to help." Well, today America is coming to help.

Let me take you to the movies.
Can I take you to the show?

Run Charlie!

Charlie don't surf!

Charlie don't surf and we think he should

Charlie don't surf and you know that it ain't no good

What is that noise now? What is the wind doing? Nothing again nothing. *Do you know nothing? Do you see nothing? Do you remember nothing?* What are the roots that clutch, what branches grow Out of this stony rubbish? Son of man, You cannot say, or guess, for you know only A heap of broken images, where the sun beats.

Ezra Pound who edited The Wasteland, he said all ages are contemporaneous right? And our job as poets and artists is to make things new, take The Odyssey or even later stuff, like even The Wasteland now, take all these old poems and make them vital again by realizing the vitality already in them. If we were able to do that, that's awakening *to* the cycle. I don't know if it's not maybe a matter of awakening *out of* the cycle, it's just awakening *to* the cycle.

Here, said she, Is your card, the drowned Phoenician Sailor. (Those are pearls that were his eyes. Look!) Here is Belladonna, the Lady of the Rocks, the lady of situations. Here is the man with three staves, and here the Wheel, And here is the one-eyed merchant.

What's your problem?   What shall we do tomorrow? O O O O What shall we ever do?   I said what is your problem?   What is your major malfunction numbnuts! Didn't mommy and daddy show you enough attention when you were a child?

And so I think what Joyce is pointing to is let's look at the whole cycle. And if we look at the whole cycle, all of these things happen simultaneously right? That's when we do, we can have Christ and Antichrist happening at once where you can have the revolution and the total tyranny happening at once as well. All of these things are happening at once. It's not... I'm not really talking about this ultimate liberation or anything, I'm just, I'm... Unless that's what the ultimate liberation is, is a matter of seeing all times and spaces at once.

And this card,

Which is blank, is something he carries on his back,

Which I am forbidden to see.

I remember

Those are pearls that were his eyes.

It's all about the Tarot sequence again, just like I said, in my Sync Book piece. And his name's literally 'Trump' so it all comes back to the Tarot sequence. But Alan you called all of this back in 2011 with the Correspondents' Dinner where Obama had his birth certificate—

> Oh thank you! Jason I want to kiss you so hard right now.

That's where it all started.

> Yes. And you're the only person who realizes how fucking poignant that is. It's insanity! It is fucking insanity.

What's?

Right because Obama had just killed Osama bin Ladin who was his previous doppelganger. So then he confronts Donald Trump who is his next doppelganger. And so we have this whole thing where we have these two eternally quarreling brothers where it's like the king becomes his shadow self in the great Joseph Campbell 'Mono Myth' cycle. So it's like first we have George Bush fighting Osama bin Ladin and Saddam Hussein and then he turns into Hussein Obama, and so then Hussein Obama starts fighting Donald Trump before he just becomes Donald Trump as the eternally revolving king on the wheel of revolution.

> Looking at that detail now, I feel idiotic for not realizing that Trump would get it.

Right cause that whole thing, that whole dinner was just Obama making fun of Donald Trump. And how ridiculous it would be if Donald Trump actually became president.

> This is when Donald Trump is leveling charges against Barack Obama, for his whole birth certificate thing.

I am releasing my official birth video.

> Nants ingonyama bagithi Baba.
> [Here comes a lion, Father]

It's this progressive shadow integration. Obama was Bush's shadow, then Donald Trump is Obama's shadow.

It's the Circle of Life And it moves us all

Say what you will about Mr Trump he certainly would bring some change to the White House. See what we've got up there.

> The week before, one week before was Easter. Right, the day that Jesus is to rise from the grave. This is the rebirth of the king. Then on Wednesday, Barack Obama introduces his birth certificate which is essentially a symbolic rebirth himself. Course the day before, Friday, is the Alchemical 'royal wedding' over there in England, very important also, but we don't have time to get into that. On Saturday, Barack Obama does his Press Correspondents' Dinner where he says 'I'm not only gonna show you my birth certificate I'm gonna show you a video of my live birth.' And he shows a video from Disney's Lion King showing this lion being held up. So not only is he announcing himself as the newborn king—you have Easter reborn king, Wednesday introducing birth certificate, Saturday showing himself as the born king and then on Sunday reports that he killed Osama bin Ladin. In Arabic, "Osama" means "lion"— in Japanese it means "king." So here you have Barack Obama presenting himself as the Lion King, saying 'I've killed the Lion King, I am the Lion King.' The king is dead, long live the king. Now if this is high occult politics or this is crazy synchronicity—

It's something.

It's definitely something, for sure.

It's like the space shuttle blows up every fucking day. How can you care about anything when you know every goddamn thing? I'm getting over one cop shooting and then another one happens, and then another one happens and another one happens. I'm crying about Paris and then Brussels happens. I can't keep track all this shit. You just give the fuck up. That's the hallmark of your generation. And that's fucked up because your generation lives in the most difficult time in human history.

Are there any queers in the theater tonight

Get em up against the wall

Ladies and gentlemen the President of the United States.

Fellow Americans...

Get him out!

A real nice place to raise your kids up.

Are you from Mexico? Are you from Mexico?

And that one looks Jewish

And that one's a coon

Who let all this riff raff

Into the room?

Get him out of here! Get out!

There's one smoking a joint And another with spots

I know it's hard to defend an unpopular policy...

If I had my way

I'd have all of them shot

Jumping

From

One

Box

Over

Into

Another

Box.

Well that was an Oedipal moment!   Sophocles?
Oedipus Tyrannus?   The guy plucks his own eyes
out! Read a book!

> Traditionally, the man who killed the king would
> take his place. Thus on that fateful Good Friday in
> April as soon as John Wilkes Booth had killed the
> king he took on the king's leg injury, symbolically
> taking his place.

Christ wasn't killed 2000 years ago,
he was killed right now.

> Yeah, every time you sit down to have your lunch.

What year is this?

This is the age of spin, the age where nobody knows what
the fuck they're even looking at.

We try to reach higher and higher resolutions but it's never the actual thing. It's just representations. It's just descriptions of what you're trying to say.

Right and here you have Los Angeles as your 'uncanny valley' where you've got all these beautiful images that don't have substance.

We are so distracted. What we see as important it's just so *not* important. Cause honestly I think everyone is crazy insecure. You see that kind of knee jerk reactionism. They get threatened and they lash out, it's because we have trinkets and consumer identities people can adopt to boost their own egos and project themselves into the world while on the inside they feel very small. And I'm hoping that changes someday. I don't know if I'll live to see it, but I like working towards that type of world.

That chess game is an example because you kind of, HAL tricks him into resigning and there's that whole, I could get into that in detail if you want, but he basically tricks Frank into thinking that certain moves are forced, whereas in fact they're not and gets Frank to resign. So that's one example of this idea of writing the script for someone else. And so, in the very first shots of when we look into the Discovery, Frank is being flipped, three out of the four scenes are flipped, cuts are flipped.

I don't know how You were inverted

I like to do things backwards. It is actually a habit. I tend to pick up books and read them backwards first.

Known to let the beat— MMM, Drop!

Right before Frank dies, right before he's murdered, there's a scene of him being flipped again and it's just showing how people can be controlled when you write the script for them. I think the broader picture to this is, and it's coming back to the false flag thing is that you can, for instance, 2001, a lot of people were tricked into supporting a foreign war. I mean this is another example of how someone's script can be written for them. It's like you're then just a two dimensional character within the film, if you're buying into this false flag story that someone else is writing for you. And the whole Space Odyssey when David Bowman, when he awakens out of this script. There's some examples of that when he's drawing the pictures of the hibernation tanks. The most intricate three dimensional drawing that he makes, for one it happens to be one in which it shows the correct orientation so that he can't be flipped. At the same time when HAL asks him what he's drawing that's the one picture he doesn't show.

He flips past it.

Yeah he flips past it and it just shows him all these other childlike two dimensional drawings which is the idea that, he's not showing HAL his true intelligence, he's not showing him that he really knows what's going on here. He's playing the part like he's a character within the film but he really does know what is going on.

Does he, like Oedipus eventually come to see a higher vision? Does his blindness, like that of Oedipus finally end the cycle?

[Frightening, isn't it?]

[The cursed destiny of man]

Absolutely have to have dark in order to have light. You gotta have dark. Gotta have opposites, dark and light, light and dark continually in painting. You have light on light you have nothing. If you have dark on dark, you basically have nothing.

But what's so great about depression?

It's like in life, you've gotta have a little sadness once in a while so you know when the good times come. I'm waiting on the good times now.

The other matter though, of reversal of form that we already got onto. There is, in IBM, for example, a phrase that information overload produces pattern recognition. This is the kind of reversal I mean. When you give people too much information they instantly resort to pattern recognition. In other words, to structuring the experience. The artist, when he encounters the present is always seeking new patterns, new pattern recognition which is his task for heaven's sake. The absolute indispensability of the artist is that he alone, in the encounter with the present can give the pattern recognition. He alone has the sensory awareness necessary to tell us what our world is made of.

It'd be a bit like if you saw a Jackson Pollock painting. And then next to it you saw another one identical. That would be very shocking wouldn't it? To see another identical version of it. Because you'd realize that whereas this first one was done like that, the second one would've had to have been done with a one hair brush. There's a dichotomy between the freedom of this thing which is apparent in the look of it, and the meticulousness of the perfect copy of it it calls into play all sorts different skills and talents, it sort of tells you about another world that exists, a world of...

Carefulness
and
meticulous
and deceit as well.

I like the deceit being involved in it. It's seeing the two together that tells you, But if you saw either one of them on its own you would only see the freedom of it.

Nobody knows what the fuck they're even looking at.

The quantum world is a world of eternal flux and change and process. The world around us that we see, the table, a chair, well defined objects in space and time, we take that as being the hard and fast reality. You know, bang on the table, you feel your knuckles hurt. It makes a sound, that's reality. But for Bohm, that was a sort of surface reality. And beyond that lay something much deeper. A deeper order which he called 'the implicate order' an order of movement and flux.

MOVEMENT AND FLUX

MOVEMENT AND FLUX.

And part of what he thought was the barrier is our language that we speak, our European family of languages. We say "the cat chases the mouse" so it's very much like a Newtonian worldview where you have well defined objects in space and time interacting by fields and forces.

A lot of people don't realize
what's really going on. They
view life as a bunch of
unconnected incidents and
things. They don't realize
that there's this lattice of
coincidence that that lays on
top of everything.

This kinda thing starts haunting you. You find out that any philosophy you can invent fails to account for it.

Synchronicity isn't a theory at all, it's a word that Jung made up and pretended he had a theory to go with it, but in the scientific sense there is no theory of synchronicity—it's just a label for a phenomenon that tends to occur when you're in Depth Analysis (Freudian or Jungian), when you do a lot of LSD, or if you do a lot of Oriental meditation, or if you practice Western Kabbalistic magic. And it happens to ordinary people too, but it happens much more likely if you belong to one of those five groups. If you belong to *all five of those groups*, the synchronicities accumulate so much that you start to think, to quote Aleister Crowley, "the whole universe is an individual dealing of God with your personal soul."

That's a little metaphysical for me.

The mystical experience breaks through from the other side and then the author has to come to term with it over the course of their entire life. It's as if the experience itself is alive. It doesn't want to be interpreted once and left in a box, it wants to be engaged over and over and over again.

Boy if you want go I would not mind

But I'm not the kind of drum you play one time

Boy if you wanna go I would not mind

But I'm not the kinda drum you play one time

One time one time one time

Boy I'm not the kinda drum you play one time

One time one time one time

Boy I'm not the kinda drum you play one time

If you want to know what your subconscious is saying, it's good to learn her language.

When you play music, that's really all you're dealing with, is time. You're directly working with time. It's the key, it's the key. I think if we could understand more about time, we'll get a little more of what reality is. When you're capturing, either with film or with tape, even audio, all these moments in time stacked maybe on each other, it's a magical act for sure. There's something bizarre about it. The more you do it, I don't know it's just a good laboratory for someone who's just seeking answers you know, or seeking better questions even.

How could this happen? She told me that late one autumn day when she was at her lowest, she watched a squirrel storing up nuts for the winter. One at a time he would take them to the nest. And she thought, if that squirrel can take care of himself with the harsh winter coming on, so can I. Once I broke my problems into small pieces, I was able to carry them just like those acorns.

I think that intelligence happens at the moment when your brain is full and you have a much bigger brain than me, much bigger. You are a fucking genius quite frankly. But I don't think—you've just got too much stuff in there. You know you've got a ton of stuff in there and you've got room for more. And I think when your brain is full, basically, and it will essentially fill to the point where all of this stuff is gonna cause you to have a complete nervous breakdown. And I hope that I'm there to enjoy that, by the way, from the sidelines with a cold one. But... You're gonna create amazing work I think.

Take all your problems and rip them apart

Of the kind that is much more, that doesn't have to rely upon so many different concepts from different fields. And I mean, the thing of it is the exact same thing could be said for me and it was, the kind of thing I'm saying, I hope I haven't insulted you.

> All right sorry, sorry about that. So uhh, go back where you were. You said you wanted—

Wha— To me, oh boy, I can go right from the fact that we had a technical break down right after David accused me of sounding like a computer, I totally fucking love it!

One of these days, I'm going to cut you into little pieces.

It gets to the point where it can't, for me anyway, synchronicity, it's so strange and so, it just can't be random in a way. It feels like there's an intentionality behind it. And what it all kinda comes down to, again is that it leads to an entirely different view of history itself. We think of it as a linear natural progression from one point to another point when we don't know that at all. It feels as though it's been arranged for us in some way or is being constantly rearranged as we are reading about it.

The potential mechanism behind the Jungian notion of synchronicity has to do with the structure of time itself.

So there's sort of an image of a vine and all the Sephirot as grapes on the vine.

Mm, I like that.

And that the Ein Sof is grape juice. I don't think of it as blood and I don't think of it as alcohol. I think of it as something more benign, something more organic and something more simple. And something that is sort of between the gods and man and animal, something that can exist just on its own.

> I've sort of made the argument that the Tarot, since it's made as cards, not as you know, we've talked about it being 'the book.' But it's a book where the pages are ripped out and you can reshuffle them. This is the cut up technique right? Well essentially the grapes are the same kinda thing. If each of those grapes is to represent a Sephirah, then wouldn't it be that when you make grape juice, you put 'em all in one bucket and mash 'em together right? So essentially it's like shuffling the Tarot cards. And when you're reading him, that's basically a variation of what he's doing there is taking all the text and mushing it together in this bucket, taking every sacred aspect of the Logos, the word, and putting it into a bucket and mixing it together and seeing what kind of you know Juicy Juice you can get out of it.

I love it.

Yeah I love that Alan. I think that's like fucking dead on. Because you've destroyed the page right? You've gone molecular. It's almost as if you can just tip the book over and pour out the contents that are inside.

If you break the lines of word and image what happens, do you get free of the patterns in there? Do you create new patterns? Or are you still stuck with the same old patterns cause you're using the same words? I think all of Burroughs' cut up experiments are interesting.

My favorite is in a book called The Third Mind and it goes, "*god damn floating whorehouse, death is the navigator.*" And I have no idea what he cut up to produce those memorable lines, but I think you've got some of the greatest poetry of the 20th Century.

The cartooner takes stodgy ambiguous cartoons like Mark Trail and mixes them with stiflingly unfunny cartoons like Blondie, puts 'em together, and makes 'em funny, check it out! Look at this, huh, let's see what happened. Well Ok, here's Dagwood and he's eating a giant sandwich made out of twigs, grubs, and a tufted titmouse.

Freud says 'the unconscious doesn't know that it's mortal' and Crowley says 'the unconscious is aware of its immortality.' That whole kind of theme. So Zeno's Paradox, right? The one about the arrow, it's just the classic, is that there's a place in your mind that you can go where you live in the moment of Zeno's Paradox which would be the arrow is your life and the bulls eye is death and the arrow never reaches the bulls eye, correct? Because it has to go half of the distance and half of the distance and then half of the distance. And mathematically you can keep that arrow in the air forever. Therefore it's immortal.

So you're saying take an asymptotic line and extend it outward?

What is that?

You've only gone halfway. You don't get to die on the cross and leave the heavy lifting to the masses. You don't get to get on stage yell wake up then just leave.

I think what the whole crazy Alex Jones, David Icke, Michael Tsarion, et cetera thing is it's kind of like the ego's own version of Jnana yoga in a way. Cause it is yoga, you're basically— yoga of the intellect, where you're connecting dots and you're exercising that faculty which is an amazing faculty that we have. And the energetic you get out of it, but it's manipulating a drive that we all have for understanding. And you have a sense that you understand but it's still superficial because you're just seeing how all the egos connect basically, which is all a fucking coping mechanism to chase the fear of death.

Stop!
Hammertime

Sync is difficult because of that because it's so indefinable.
I mean we use the word sync but it really doesn't—

That's its strength, that's its strength.

It's everywhere.

Right.

If you look, you're syncing all your devices all the time.

It's the study of Tao. It's fucking indescribable.

You know, you can't touch that, it's taboo. Why, so I
don't know, you have to be able to draw your own
lines in these situations and not be intimidated
about being a little crazy.

Sure.

This could be a case of group hypnosis. Was there
really a house? Was there actually a Mrs Baker? Or
was it all some kind of dream?

It was no dream. **This is really happening!**

Cultures before us, all over the world, they always used synchronicity. They used reading nature to live in harmony with each other live in harmony with the environment. They lived much saner lives.

> Mystics definitely have a certain practice that sustains them or rejuvenates them. You're interesting to me in that you have more of a scientific practice. Like a—a natural philosopher from days of yore where they're interacting with reality and trying to understand the nature of it. Where science and alchemy were one and the same. What does your practice look like?

I think science is basically a magic. It's a form of magic, it's a form of mysticism, like you just said, it was born out of alchemy. From that angle it's just another way of divination, really what are scientists trying to do? They're trying to predict stuff. So they find all these laws, quote unquote, where they piece them together through their runes, you know they assemble their runes, their symbols, and it divines some event. And then they all celebrate. It's very much just a magical ritual that they seem to be reenacting if you really want to get down to the root level of it. And that's all man does is they just find new ways of reenacting magical ritual.

Two frames is too much.

Following total atomic annihilation, the rebuilding of this great nation of ours may fall to you. In this chapter we focus on perception.

Joyce also compares... It's hard to say compares, he uses the metaphor of Humpty Dumpty. Humpty Dumpty falling off the wall. And I think you can use Humpty Dumpty as sort of a metaphor for Western history in a way. You have Humpty Dumpty on the wall and this is tradition. The old style Medieval tradition where there was a sort of metaphysical foundation to things. And then you have Humpty Dumpty falling off the wall which is the death of God where everything becomes adrift. *Adrift. Adrift.* Adrift in Nietzsche's terms. There's not a foundation to anything anymore. And so then you have the sort of shattered fragments of the, of Humpty Dumpty's eggshells, and then the king's horses and the king's men try to put Humpty together again. And this is the modernist project of trying to create something, a brand new tradition out of scratch. To make it as foundational as the old traditions. But hopefully, hopefully freer or wiser or whatever. And ultimately that project fails. And then there's sort of this post-modern phase where it's instead of trying to rebuild, people are just playing with the fragments of the eggshells, just playing with the pieces. This is what Jean Baudrillard called it. But then finally we reach a stage after that of, this is where ALP comes in, where the pieces just self-organize themselves. There's this period of emergence, and I think that's where sync comes in as well. It's kind of this... Post post-modern moment. I don't know if that sounds crazy but something new is coming in with this right? And I think it comes in with the whole structure of the internet itself which is almost foreshadowed by Finnegan's Wake according to Marshall McLuhan.

And that's like the chicken that Marshall McLuhan writes about. Where they took this film to these tribal people in Africa and they were gonna teach them about water safety so they show 'em this five minute film on how to appropriately collect water so that the water wasn't filled with disease or some shit. And they asked the tribal people, what did you see in the movie? The only thing that they could all agree on was that they saw a chicken. And the filmmakers were puzzled they said there's no chicken in the movie. And everyone that they screened it to said that they saw a chicken. So they went back and they slowed down the film and looked at it frame by frame and for less than a second and a half a chicken runs across a bottom corner of the film screen.

Two frames is too much.

This is something that they, they couldn't see, they literally could not see it until they slowed down the film and looked at it frame by frame, but this is something that every single tribal person, it leapt out of them out of the screen. It was the only thing that they really had any absolute sense of was that, oh there's a chicken flying across the wall. So this is Kubrick's playing with the edges of our consciousness and playing with our dimensions of literacy. He's embedding within every inch of his films differing layers of perception. And it's all these different layerings of perception that agitate our unconscious and our conscious so much.

The alchemists had two components to their philosophy. These were the principles of Solve and Coagula. Solve was basically the equivalent of analysis. It was taking things apart to see how they work. Coagula was basically synthesis. It was trying to put the disassembled pieces back together so that they worked more efficiently. There is recently, in literature for example, been a wave of post-modernism, deconstructionism. This is Solve. Perhaps it is time in the arts for a little more Coagula. Having deconstructed everything, perhaps we really should be starting to think about putting everything back together.

Two households both alike in dignity in fair Verona where we lay our scene. From ancient grudge break to new mutiny. Where civil blood makes civil hands unclean. From forth the fatal loins of these two foes a pair of star crossed lovers take their life whose misadventured piteous overthrows doth with their death bury their parents' strife. The fearful passage of their death-mark'd love, And the continuance of their parents' rage, Which, but their children's end, nought could remove. Is now the two hours' traffic of our stage.

The idea

Exactly.

The idea is that Ferris Bueller—

Trivial trivial.

Ferris Bueller doesn't exist. Ferris Bueller is totally a figment of—

Cameron's imagination.

Cameron's imagination.

I believe it 100% you don't even have to say another word. Yeah. Holy shit.

And what's her name, Sloane too is also, the whole thing is in Cameron's head. He never gets out of bed.

I believe it. Yeah. That's the thing it doesn't matter but because that's such an acceptable spin—

You can totally watch it that way.

It's an acceptable spin on that—

You can totally watch it that way.

On that Ur-phenomena whatever you want to call it.

You know all of this business of, are these interpretations real or are they not, you know, the question of did the original artist intend it is an interesting one. But it's not necessarily the definitive question. Whether they intended it or not, it's cool to watch it that way.

It's weird because that's how my dial was turned up. So I remember watching Fight Club for the first time and being like what the fuck was that? And they're like, nothing was there dude, what are you talking about? I was like no, there was a person just flashed on screen. Have you seen that in Fight Club?

The Dick?

No they actually put Tyler Durden, you know how he puts the dick in the movie for a quick second? Before he's even introduced, they flip him in the movie three times. And my fucking eye caught it. And everybody's like nothing's there dude, nothing's there.

We don't mind being blindfolded.

Right, blindfolds on.

What's that?

Merely sound effects Robin, recorded on tape by talented professional thespians.

Brought to its logical conclusion, such a physiological habitus becomes an instinctive hatred of all reality, a flight into the intangible, into the incomprehensible. A distaste taste for all formula, for all conceptions of time and space, for everything established, customs, institutions, the church, a feeling of being at home in a world which no sort of reality survives, a merely inner world, a true world, an eternal world. The kingdom of God is within you.

> In the meantime, you have Babylon. It invests everything into basically making a name for itself, or shem for itself to quote the Old Testament, right? So Babylon builds itself according to these parameters but it's a mandala and it's not built to last. Yet at the same time I can recognize even in myself when I fucking put my blog together and my name isn't attributed to it or it's mixed up into a heap of other peoples' info I wanna distinguish. I want to be like no, these are my thoughts. And then we have why the fucking whole copyright thing and all this stuff where is that really coming from? And does it have anything to do with—beyond us looking for reference points in order to localize our sense of self which is completely holographic and has no basis in reality the same way that Babylon is in the first place as being completely holographic and having no basis in reality? So anyways.

The instinctive hatred of reality. The consequence of an extreme—

It's like a kid on a slide in a playground. They're afraid to go down the slide. Once they get to the bottom, they want to go right back up again and do it again.

To me, one of the problems with the analysis of literature is that it generally proceeds exactly like a book or a story does, it's a linear thing. You take an idea and then you carry it to its so-called touchdown. I like to use that sports metaphor. But really the Shining, the work of Kubrick is multi-dimensional so you can carry an idea to a direct and correct conclusion and then still have a million other correct conclusions that you could also come to.

I guess it's part of that constant challenge of being willing to use media that compromise the message in a way that is fair trade off, that the media itself can somehow be transformed if only temporarily by the message that's going through it.

There is a challenge about writing because of what SJ was saying about language that there's something about language which actually disassociates us from reality and in and of itself.

So there's this, I think it's a really exciting time to try to use language to achieve the very thing that language has actually kind of prevented us from experiencing, which is intimacy.

McLuhan, in a great lecture by McKenna, McKenna relates this. He says you don't *Look* at a book, you *Read* it. And so when you open the book you're not looking anymore, you're doing this particular function of your visual senses right? And when you read the book and then you put the book down and you look up, you're still doing that reading thing. Your visual senses are still in that mode and so your hearing, your tasting and your feeling they're not at the levels that they should be.

Lift your head out of the film, lift your head out of the TV, lift your head out of the book and then sync in your daily life.

I just thought it was so
interesting put those two
conversations side by side.

It deliberately broke down.

I mean, what are we really talking about here right?

It deliberately broke down!

I just have to document the absurdity of existence before it fritters away.

So that's important.

That's how I stay sane.

His whole thing is that when sex dies, it becomes climax. When play dies it becomes The Game.

Children with their imagination, it's so expansive, so open, and then as that dies it gets translated into this game and everyone's playing the fucking massive game that's basically killing itself.

It's a breakdown. He's looking at his whole act in that light, what was play has turned into the game and so the best he can do is end it in the best way possible.

It is a breakdown, basically. Obviously it's a part of a process. And I'm not a Buddhist in the sense that I hold out hope basically, for an actual permanent, potentially permanent, but at least satisfying, some kind of resolution to all this. I'm not sure what that's going to be and I wouldn't dare speculate on it.

In association with
Apophenia Productions
and
FairUseVideos.org

Bill Klaus

David Plate

Alan Green

Douglas Bolles

Will Morgan

John Maguire

Andras Jones

Guillaume Samard

Wally Scharold

M.G.

Kay Pax

Alex Fulton

SJ Anderson

Dennis Koch

Patrick Sevc

JJ Draa

TheSyncBook.com presents

A film by Alan Green

Featuring:

Mark LeClair

Dr Eric McLuhan

Jason Barrera

Znore

Joe Alexander

Jake Kotze

JJ McAdams

Matt Pulver

Christine M Grimm

Jon Kidd

Matthew Guggemos

Camile de Toledo

Rodney Ascher

Mark Hosler

Rabbi Borukh Goldberg

David Peat

Gary Lachman

Nancy McMoneagle

Dr Jeffrey Kripal

John Fell Ryan

Paul Levy

Steve Willner

Sibyl Hunter

Ben Goraj

Jasun Horsley

Michael Isaiah

Michael Schacht

Featuring:

Stanley Kubrick

Marshall McLuhan

T. S. Eliot

Dave Chappelle

Werner Herzog

Norman Jordan

Twin Peaks

Bob Ross

I Heart Huckabees

Pink Floyd

Brian Eno

William S. Burroughs

René Magritte

Alan Moore

Sonic Outlaws

Timothy Leary

Lucifer Rising

Jeffrey Mishlove

Robert Anton Wilson

Terence McKenna

Featuring:

A Lefthanded Fingerpainting - The Donkeys
The Vaporous Bridge To Stellar Window - Steve Willner
The Bridge Over Jim Carrey - Jon Kidd
The Two Mothers - Borukh Goldberg & Patrick Sevc
Heartbreak [Everything's Jake] - Christopher North
Back to the Future Predicts 9/11 - Joe Alexander
Room 237 - Rodney Ascher
San Francisco - Anthony Stern
Week Tripper - Zach Bauer

Mystery Behind - Andras Jones
Jennifer Jupiter - Jake Kotze
Nosis - Jim Sanders
2001afalseflagodyssey - Matt Pulver & Patrick Sevc
The Shining: Forwards and Backwards - John Fell Ryan
Donald Trump's The Wall - In The Flesh
Brain Phase 1 - Jordan Bartee
The Twilight Zone [The Fever, Elegy, Mirror Image]
Corbett Report - James Corbett
Unplug – Beeple

Would love to be able to credit the people who made the videos mixed in at 18:00-18:12 and 50:46-51:38, the animation from 37:33-38:15, as well as the Clarebow drone at 1:15:03

Ideas are hard to own and slices of culture even more so. Time will prove us all fools, but for now:

COPYRIGHTED MATERIAL REMAINS THE PROPERTY OF ITS RESPECTIVE OWNERS AND IS USED IN ACCORDANCE WITH THE PRINCIPLES OF FAIR USE

Appologies for any credit I forgot or missed

8 ½

2010

200-Motels

A Beautiful Mind

An Andalusian Dog

Apocalypse Now

Aronofsky's Pi

A$Ap Mob - Yamborghini High

Back To The Future I & II

Barton Fink

Battle Of Olympus [NES]

Beastie Boys - Intergalactic

Belladonna Of Sadness

Black Moon

Brazil

Brian Springer's Spin

Cake - Arco Arena

Cake - Cool Blue Reason

Capricorn One

Chameleon Street

Clash Of The Titans

Contact

Cowboy Bebop Soundtrack

Cut Chemist - Metrorail Thru Space

Dave Matthews - So Much To Say

Dave Mckean's The Week Before

David Bowie - Blackstar

Depeche Mode - Enjoy The Silence

Donnie Darko

Dumbo

El Topo

Eurythmics - Sweet Dreams

EVA Pod Ambient Sound - crysknife007

Everly Brothers - Dream

Everything Must Go - Ion

Explorers

Fear And Loathing In Las Vegas

Flash Gordon

Fleetwood Mac - The Chain

Forrest Gump

Frank Zappa - Lumpy Gravy

Fred Myro & Malcom Seagrave - Phantasm Theme

Funeral Parade Of Roses

Futurama

Gumby

Hall & Oates - I Can't Go For That

Hirokazu Tanaka - Kid Icarus Theme

Hugo

Ipod Ads

James Brown - Blind Man Can See It

Jerry Goldsmith: Logan's Run Soundtrack
John Dies At The End
John Searl: Law Of Squares
Jon Brion - I Heart Huckabees Soundtrack
Knight Of Cups
Kung Fury
Led Zeppelin - Houses Of The Holy
Link Wray - Rumble
Little Nemo: Adventures In Slumberland
Look Who's Talking
Lord Of The Rings
Lou Reed - Rouge
Marian Hill - One Time
Marv Newland's Black Hula
Mary Ellen Bute's Passages from James Joyce's Finnegans Wake
Mc Hammer - Can't Touch This
Meatloaf - Wasted Youth
Me!Me!Me!
Menahan Street Band - Seven Is The Wind
Miles Davis - Blue In Green
Millennium
Mr Bill Safety Tips
Mst3k: Manos The Hands Of Fate
National Anthem - NAOMI19631963
Neil Young - Dead Man Theme
Nico - These Days
Nine Inch Nails - Closer
Osamu Tezuka's Metropolis
Pan's Labyrinth
PARADISE - Studio SmackAdaptation
Patrick & Ralph Carney - Bojack Horseman Opening Theme
Peter David Connelly - The Radio8Ball show
Poky Little Puppy
Portishead - Undenied
Powers Of Ten
Puzzling Evidence [True Stories]
Qavor - Nausicaä [Hip Hop Beat]
Radiohead - Hunting Bears [800mix]
Radiohead - Push Pull Revolving Doors
Ratatat - Cherry
Ray Charles - I Can't Stop Loving You
Repo Man
Rod Stewart - Amazing Grace
Rodney Ascher's The S From Hell
Romeo + Juliet
Rosemary's Baby
Salome's Last Dance
Slaughterhouse Five
Star Wars
Stranger Things

Suicide Kings - Alan Abbadessa-Green
Svankmajer's Darkness Light Darkness
Talking Heads - Psycho Killer [Live]
The Beatles - Can You Take Me Back
The Beatles - Revolution 9
The Beatles - While My Guitar Gently Weeps [Demo]
The Clash - Charlie Don't Surf
The Creation [Strana Mechty] - Stories From The Bible
The Cure - A Forest
The Dark Knight
The Dot and the Line: A Romance in Lower Mathematics
The Dynamic Scooby Doo Affair
The Guess Who - American Woman
The Holy Mountain
The Legend of Zelda
The Life Aquatic With Steve Zissou
The Matrix
The Ninth Configuration
The Parallax View
The Royal Tenenbaums
The Shadow
The Simpsons
The Sixth Sense
The Terminator
The Third Man
The Tick
The Truman Show
The Visitor
The White Stripes - Little Acorns
The White Stripes - There's No Home For You Here
The Who - Tommy [Album]
The Who - Won't Get Fooled Again [Live]
The Xx - Intro
Thee Oh Sees - Penetrating Eye
Theory of Ghostplane - CollinAlexander
They Live
They Might Be Giants - Birdhouse In Your Soul
They Might Be Giants - Subliminal
Turkish man yelling "meow" at an egg - Christoffer Bader
Twin Peaks: Fire Walk With Me
Utopic Music
Wax Tailor - Hypnosis Theme
Weird Voicemail From Flight 370
White House Correspondents' Dinner: Lion King
Willy Wonka and the Chocolate Factory
Yellow Submarine
Yes - Roundabout
Zardzoz
Zelda II: The Adventure of Link

Archival Cavalry:

Keith Zavatski

Douglas Bolles
Will Morgan
Jay Action
Zach Bauer
Patrick Sevc
Guillaume Samard
Kay Pax
Jim Kincaid
Dennis Koch
Alan Waller
Ben Brujo
Oli Dunlop

VISION AND THE VOICE

Watch the film at
TheSyncBook.com/VAV

9 7 9 8 6 7 6 6 3 5 1 5 2